A CHUDLEIGH Collection

COMPILED BY THE CHUDLEIGH AMENITY SOCIETY
WITH THE HELP OF CHIPS BARBER

OBELISK PUBLICATIONS

Other Books in this Series

Albert Labbett's Crediton Collection
Albert Labbett's Crediton Collection II
An Alphington Album, *P. Aplin & J. Gaskell*
The Dawlish Collection, *Bernard Chapman*
The Totnes Collection, *Bill Bennett*
Peter Tully's Pictures of Paignton
Peter Tully's Pictures of Paignton Part II
Ian Jubb's Exeter Collection
Mike & Hilary Wreford's Okehampton Collection
Mike & Hilary Wreford's Okehampton Collection II
Fred Tozer's Newton Abbot Album
Pictorial Torquay, *Leslie Retallick*
Kingsteignton Collection, *Richard Harris*
A Brixham Album
An Exeter Boyhood, *Frank Retter*

Some Other Obelisk Publications

The Lost City of Exeter, Chips Barber
Diary of a Devonshire Walker, *Chips Barber*
Made in Devon, *Chips Barber and David FitzGerald*
Tales of the Teign, *Chips Barber and Judy Chard*
Tales of the Unexplained in Devon, *Judy Chard*
Haunted Happenings in Devon, *Judy Chard*
The Ghosts of Exeter, *Sally and Chips Barber*
The Templer Way, *Derek Beavis*
The Magic Triangle, *Deryck Seymour*
The Secret Square, *Deryck Seymour*
Ashburton of Yesteryear, *John Germon & Pete Webb*
Around & About Teignmouth & Shaldon, *Chips Barber*
Dartmoor in Colour, *Chips Barber*
Beautiful Exeter, *Chips Barber*
Torbay in Colour, *Chips Barber*
Plymouth in Colour, *Chips Barber*

Acknowledgements

Thanks to all those who helped in getting the collection together, especially to Eddie Lee, former town clerk, and Christopher Pidsley, vicar, who both lent photographs and helped a lot by giving additional information concerning the Society's collection. Also to Patrick G. Radford for the use of his pictures.
The Society would be pleased to receive any additional information or photos etc. for their collection, so they may preserve 'Chudleigh of the past' for future generations.

Patricia Bounds
Chudleigh Amenity Society

For further details of these or any of our extensive Devon titles, please contact us at 2 Church Hill, Pinhoe, Exeter, EX4 9ER, Tel: (0392) 468556.

First Published in 1994 by Obelisk Publications
2 Church Hill, Pinhoe, Exeter, Devon
Designed by Chips and Sally Barber
Typeset by Sally Barber
Printed in Great Britain by
Ashley House, Marsh Barton, Exeter

ISBN: 0 946651 89 2

This book is a nostalgic look back at Chudleigh as it was in the past. The collection of photographs has been assembled by members of The Chudleigh Amenity Society and an attempt has been made to include a variety of views and a number of familiar faces and places. We hope that you will enjoy looking back and that you will find something of personal interest. This view of Fore Street is taken at a time when the pace of life was a lot slower, even in Chudleigh! The shop on the left with the name 'King' just discernible is now Gill's the greengrocer and the large house next to it was used, during the First World War, as a hospital for convalescing troops.

4

Fore Street, Chudleigh

Although Chudleigh is well served for shops today, at one time there were far more than there are now. Had you built a wall around Chudleigh early in the twentieth century you would have found that the town was self-sufficient with all the trades and professions well represented. In particular Chudleigh was well blessed with pubs and inns but these two pictures show the shop that simply traded under the name 'Kelly'. Apart from jugs, Kelly's specialised in selling glass and china, something they did for a great many years, "Established since the time of Milton." Today Miss Kelly's shop, "The Big Jug", is no longer a shop. Some of the painted jugs are still above the windows as a reminder of its former glorious past.

This picture shows us a bit more of the street and is taken in about 1930. Despite the fact that this was, at the time of the photograph, one of the main roads in England, it was still very quiet on the afternoon that this picture was taken.

Farther down Fore Street and a little closer to Plymouth was The Plymouth Inn, one of many in the county to bear this name. However things change and today the inn, which is believed to be haunted, is now The Bishop Lacy. The view was one captured and published by the celebrated postcard firm of Chapman & Son of Dawlish.

7

After the trauma and tragedy of the First World War it is entirely understandable that the Armistice, in 1918, would be greeted with great rejoicings throughout the land. In Chudleigh it was no different as shops garlanded in flags and bunting were the norm. The shop on the left is now Chudleigh News (Garbett's) and the one on the right is Avanti Hair Design, once Edwards the tailors.

A large crowd gathered in The Square for a ceremony in honour of King George V and Queen Mary. Because of the limited nature of photography at that time those people who were moving, when the picture was being taken, are blurred. However the jockey on the right appears to be static enough! The bell tower on the Town Hall has since been removed.

The above photograph dates back to 1907 and is another view from the prolific publishers of Chapman and Son of Dawlish. In the background is a line of shops that run from the former "Reading Matters" bookshop up to the corner of Clifford St where Taylor's Ship Hotel, now the Ship Inn, is sited. In between are shops belonging to Saunders and also to Norman.
The view opposite is also of The Square but taken from a different angle. It shows the fountain in full flow and the long departed Lion Inn. Note the hoops hanging on the shop next door.

Not the merest hint of a motor car in sight in the picture above, again taken in The Square. This time we look up Old Exeter Road. On the left is a shoe shop and beyond that a newsagents. Some of the buildings on the left, just beyond the lad with crutches, were pulled down. This is the entrance to the health centres and main car park, the site of a former farmhouse and orchard. On the right a single signpost informs us that the way to Exeter is to the right. The bank on the corner and the Lion Inn next door to it became so unsafe that they had to be demolished and now it is a garden with an open prospect that enhances the scene. The bank owns and maintains the site.

The photo on the opposite page presents a good contrast with the first cars seen in the district getting a lot of attention. Lord Clifford is shown here being chauffeur-driven into The Square.

The White Hart Hotel is a business that remains despite the passage of many years. The shadows indicate that this picture is taken in the morning and a fine one at that as the hotel has its first floor window wide open. Next door Powlesland and Son have boards, outside their newsagent's shop, stating the headlines of the day.

The photograph on the opposite page is of the ceremony, in May 1926, to dedicate the War Memorial and the large crowd have put on their 'Sunday Best' to attend. Sadly most of the crowd will have known several people killed in the conflict, making this a poignant ceremony for them. The building and gateway close to the Town Hall have since been demolished.

The Highwayman's Haunt, on the former A38, just outside Chudleigh is well known in this part of Devon and derives its name from the highwayman, Jack Withrington, who was eventually caught and executed on the gallows at Tyburn in 1691. These two photos are of that building in the days when it was called 'Rowells' and was the family home of the Cobley family. The picture on the opposite page is believed to have been taken in about 1888 and is an unusual family picture.

These fine upstanding men are posed for the camera at Hamlyn's Farm (Whiteway Estate). A great variety of headwear is being sported by the men who have taken a little time out from hay-making to be captured for immortality. In the back row are Mr Pomeroy (bailiff), Mr Pomeroy junior, E. Sanders (coachman and grandfather of well-known local man Eddie Lee), two estate workers and T. Burnett(shepherd). In the front row are Mr Blackmoor, J. Townsend, J. Cobley, Mr Richards, Mr Cobley junior and an unknown labourer.

From the surrounding countryside we go back to Chudleigh and a gathering of a different kind. Here we have a group assembled in the old Vicarage garden, now "The Glebe House". It was taken in about 1928 and it is just about possible to make out the church tower on the right hand side of the picture. So many years on it is difficult to identify everyone in the photo but the back row includes, in order from left to right, Dr H. Walters, B. Tompkin, M. Robertson, (Unknown), S. Clampit, Mrs Heywood, (another unknown), A. Holcombe, Mrs R. Cox, Frank Hellier (who owned the bank and the pub buildings that were demolished in The Square), Mrs Martin, Mrs Stephens, W. Lang, (another unknown), J. Page, S. Cobley and W. Pearce. The front row included Mrs Malder, Colonel Platt, (Unknown), R. Ellis, Major Harvey (Conservative MP for the Totnes Division), Mrs Harvey, M, Nosworthy, J. Webber, who was a headmaster and another unknown. Apologies to those whom we couldn't name!

In about 1930 Chudleigh got a new church clock and this excellent photo shows the group of men entrusted with the task of hoisting it into position. By a quick examination of their names it seems that it was almost a prerequisite that one needed to be either called "Bill" or "Sam" in those days! Only a single "Walter" breaks the pattern. In the photograph we have Bill and Walter Shapley raised at the back and, from left to right, Bill Cornish, Sam Rowlands, Sam Blackmore, Bill Gordon and Bill Bolt at the front.
The picture opposite is how Chudleigh Church looked about the year 1900.

Here is a photograph, taken in about 1930, of Mr A. W. Brooking who was Chudleigh's station master, for a great many years. In those days even small country stations were staffed. There was a time when it was possible to reach almost any town or village in the county by rail. Chudleigh was on the Teign Valley line, a route that offered an alternative way of travelling between Exeter and Newton Abbot. The line left Exeter, and the main line, just south of Exeter St Thomas Station and curved gracefully above fields that are now the Marsh Barton Trading Estate. It passed the small Alphington Halt, a hut on a single wooden platform, to turn along the valley of the Alphin Brook. At Ide the line contoured the hillside above the village and headed on through the densely wooded Perridge. Longdown Station was the next stop, one sandwiched between two tunnels. Dunsford Halt was the last stopping place before reaching the Teign Valley. Following this natural corridor southwards there were further stations at Christow, Ashton and Trusham with the line crossing the River Teign four times, before Chudleigh Station was reached. The trains passed slowly along this line and beyond Chudleigh continued to Chudleigh Knighton and on to Heathfield. Here it joined the Moretonhampstead to Newton Abbot line.

The Teign Valley line was never prosperous, possibly because it ran along the valley bottom and the villages, which it served, were high on the hillsides above! So when the axe fell on rural railways this one was bound to be a victim. The last train passed along the line on 7 June 1958.

The picture on the opposite page predates 'wheely-bins' and was probably published as a bit of fun.

For railway enthusiasts this double page spread of pictures showing Chudleigh's former railway station must be 'just the ticket'! On this page is evidence that there are occasionally disadvantages in building a railway along a river valley, in this case the River Teign. The picture was taken on 5 December 1929. However the smiling faces of the passengers 'waiting' for the train, which presumably would have been cancelled, suggests that they weren't being too serious. There is little trace of the station now as the A38 runs along the line of the railway. The slip road leading down to the dual carriageway passes over what was the station sidings.

24

CHUDLEIGH RAILWAY STATION

The modes of transport are different and the roofing materials have changed but these two scenes of Coburg Corner are clearly recognisable despite the gulf of many years. The two pictures are included so that you can play a version of 'spot the difference.' This sort of change has been repeated in towns and villages the length and breadth of the country. Earlier this century there was a fire here that caused much damage,

a large crowd turning out to watch it at its height. Had the right side of it not had a corrugated roof, the damage would have been far worse! Mr Buttress lived here and was a wheelwright, his workshops being in the buildings to the right of the picture. They have since been turned into houses.

Here we have another pair of past and present photographs. The one on this page is taken in about the year 1900 whereas the one opposite is more modern. The views both show "The Laurels" in the foreground but the one on this page is a country scene of fields, with the church on the skyline. The upper field to the right of the church is where the new school is built, the other a more urban scene showing the steady

growth of Chudleigh. Located between Newton Abbot and Exeter, and close to a major road, it is perfectly sited for anyone prepared to motor to work. The days have long since passed when the bulk of the people who live in Chudleigh work there as well. Let's hope that Chudleigh isn't just a place to sleep in but remains a lively and active community, a place with a sense of pride and belonging.

Limestone is such a versatile rock. It can be used for building, road construction and, in the past, it was burnt to be used as a sweetener to improve farm soils. Not only that but it often forms gorges with cliff-like slopes that can be climbed and underground caverns, which can be explored by speliologists. There is plenty of this rock at Chudleigh and its potential has been fully explored. In this photograph we can see Glen Cottage with Palace Quarry behind. In past times teas were served in the orchard at Glen Cottage to visitors who came from Exeter and surrounding towns to view the famous Chudleigh Rocks, caves and waterfall.

This is an unfamiliar view of Lawrence Castle, better known to locals as Haldon Belvedere. The picture is taken a great many years ago for now it has far more woodland in its vicinity. The tower is a familiar landmark for anyone who drives over The Haldon Hills and the view from the top of it is one of the best in Devon with views over Dartmoor, East Devon, South Devon, up to Exmoor and across to Somerset. It appears that the track leading up to it was known as "The Processional Way."

One of the activities that is still carried out on a regular basis is the beating of the bounds. Long before the days of maps and motorised traffic this was done so that the older members of the community, who had done the trek many times, could pass on, to the younger ones, the precise limits of the parish. It was also an excuse for revelry and a good time was had by all, except, of course, those unfortunates who were "bumped" on boundary stones or thrown in streams. Here we have such an event from the past with the participants all prepared, with mugs in hand, to quench their thirsts. One of the men in the centre of the picture, in front of the tree, is Albert Holcombe who owned a printing business where Choy's takeaway now is located.

A far better way to travel, than by Shanks's Pony, was by the latest in modern comfort - the charabanc! Here is a group from the local Conservative Association Committee who are indulging in a rare treat, the most likely destination for their motor outing being down to Torquay or up to Dartmoor. The open top charabanc meant that its passengers were exposed to the elements. This would account for the fact that they are dressed up to combat any adverse weather. The ladies are wearing some impressive hats and these too are well secured to their heads! A close inspection of the photograph reveals a variety of expression on these faces. The driver is standing on the running board of his vehicle and is wearing a distinctive driver's cap.

Fifteen smartly attired scouts are captured on film at the playing field alongside the old pavilion. The picture is believed to have been taken in about 1918. In the right hand background can be seen Little Hill, which is now known as James House. Although it has been impossible to name all these saintly-looking individuals, the picture includes the following: Bill Pike, Alf Cobley, Topsy Wills, Bob Taylor, George Shears, Bill Bowden and Charlie Cobley.

The Chidley Garrison Artillery are shown here in all their resplendent glory. The 'Chidley' was something of a joke at the time. It is believed that they have assembled in readiness to participate in one of Chudleigh's celebrated carnivals, possibly just after the First World War when there was great relief at the cessation of hostilities.

The Chudleigh Town Band has given a lot of people a lot of pleasure over the years and here are two pictures of them from the past. On this page they are looking very smart but do not have uniforms. However they are a young-looking bunch of men and some four years later several

of them were still around to wear the smart outfit that was adopted to give them that all important finishing touch. The man in the homburg, in the earlier photo, is George Barbour who came down to Devon from the North to train them.

This is the Chudleigh Volunteer Band and they are shown here in 1897, the year of Queen Victoria's Diamond Jubilee.

The class of 1920 at the infants school in Chudleigh. Note the bell tower which was over the entrance from Fore Street. The angelic expressions belong to the following Chudleigh cherubims, (L to R) back row: E. Lee, L. Shillabear, M. Weeks, G. Pridie, T. Bulpin, L. Parker, T. Tremeer, J. Whiteway, W. Slee, N. Hough, T. Holcombe, C. Heath, K. Welch, W. Berry, T. Hamlin. Front Row: R. Tremeer, L. Jordan, W. Watkins, L. Doble, A. Burridge, L. Phillips, J. O'Toole, T. Bulpin, T. Heath, L. Rowe, P. Adams, K. Cornish, and A. Wills. Kitchener Cornish went on to become a butcher, inheriting the business from his father, and passing it on to his own son many years later.

Only one little girl, on the far right, managed a smile for this photograph. It was taken at Chudleigh Church School in 1905 by T. Cann of Fore Street, Bovey Tracey. The lady teacher has that look of experience about her and it is hard to imagine that these children would have ever dared to step out of line in her presence! Although the style of dress dates the photograph, the hairstyles are not that far removed from those of today – apart from the teacher's.

However by 1920 this group were stepping out of line, but purely for a good cause. Here the young ladies have all raised their left legs as part of a drill they were practising at Chudleigh School.

41

Again we have some now familiar faces and names from this picture of standards 6 and 7 from Chudleigh Church School in 1927. Eddie Lee kindly lent this photo which is taken when he held the post of 'Yard Monitor'. This call to officialdom was to stay with him right through his adult life as he became Chudleigh's Town clerk, a position he held for 45 years – quite an achievement! In this picture are the following (L to R): Back Row – T. Heath, E. Holmes, E. Sampson, S. Bailey, L. Jordan, H. Offerd, K. Cornish. Middle Row – E. Lee, A. Burridge, T., Tremeer, J. Frankpitt, A. Wills, K. Welch, L. Doble, S. Davis. Front Row – P. Trout, L. Bray, C. Blackmoor, B. Hellier, J. Blackmoor, J. Middlewick and E. Kentisbear.

Our last school photo is from November 1954 and the expressions on the pupils' faces are much more animated with smiles the order of the day for this handsome bunch of Chudleigh Primary School pupils. (L to R) Back Row: G. Brimblecombe, G. Hugg, A. Taylor, Miss Smith (Teacher), D. Adams, M. Prettyjohn, D. Tuckett. Second Row: P. Trout, A. Slocombe, J. Pascoe, C. Wilson, ? Mackinson, J. James, V. Barrs. Third Row: G. Gidley, R. Hearne, J. Bradford, M. Edwards, R. Stevens, R. Grant, S. Seward. Front Row: G. Lee, R.M. Bryant, P. Mead, W. Sampson, C. Salmon.

This is a relatively modern photo and was taken in 1984. Sheep are still occasionally seen in Fore Street, which is appropriate as Chudleigh was famous, at least in Devon, as a wool town, a fact that it emphasises on its name signs on the approaches to the town. Here a large flock are seen heading past the church towards the town: the vicar heard them coming and ran for his camera to prove the point!

Pictures like the last one would have been impossible had the by-pass not been built for it has given the town back a relative peace. The thought of the volume of traffic that uses the A38 going through the town again would be a frightening one for residents. They realised their good fortune when the by-pass was opened in 1973 and staged a colourful pageant to celebrate the occasion.

Sport has always been important in Chudleigh life and the last few pictures of the book feature just some of the many faces who have represented the town. Here cricket is being played on a field that was only used for cricket and this in the months from April to September. In the background is the old pavilion that has its rather impressive grandstand, complete with spectators, on top of it. This was demolished and replaced by the present clubhouse, in 1972, that is to the left of the previous one. The Kate Brook Sports Centre now offers fine facilities for sports activities.

This is the Second XI (plus dog and umpire) as seen on cricket pitches in the neighbourhood during the 1956 season. (L to R) Back Row: Black, Massey, Davis, Unknown, Doble, Shears and Eddie Lee (Umpire). Front Row: Gilpin, Gatland, Pelmear, Newcombe and Watkins.

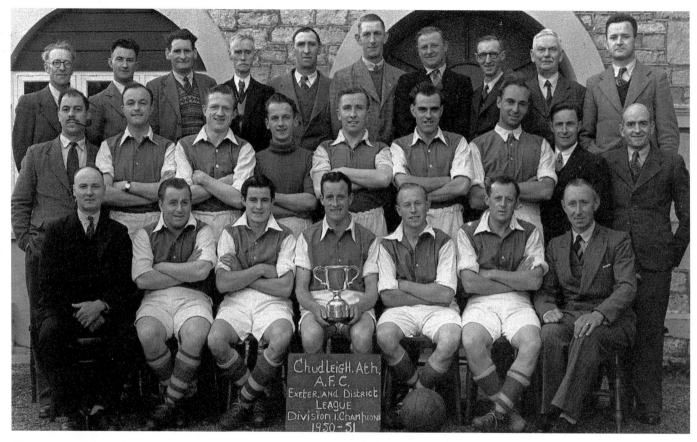

It's nice to end the book on a winning note and the board in front of the players and the proudly held trophy say it all. The roll of honour in the 1950/51 season featured the following personnel: (L to R) Back Row – E. Kentisbear, J. Bone, J. Leaman, C. Skinner, W. Northcott, W. Frome, M. Tuckett, F. Caunter, W. Wheeler, F. Campion. Middle Row – E. Davis, B. Warden, W. Kemble, F. Northcott, H. Searle, P. Doble, I. Roberts, J. Denyer, G. Cornish. Front Row – C. Coysh, H. Beckerleg, R. Watkins, S. Watkins (Capt), C. Hopkins, D. Parker and E. Lee. We hope you have enjoyed this nostalgic look at Chudleigh of yesteryear.